Late Thoughts in March

to my dearest three and Louise

John Powell Ward
Late Thoughts in March

seren

seren
is the book imprint of
Poetry Wales Press Ltd
Wyndham Street, Bridgend, Wales

© John Powell Ward, 1999

The right of John Powell Ward to be identified as the Author
of this Work has been asserted in accordance with the
Copyright, Designs and Patents Act 1988.

ISBN 1-85411-250-3

A CIP record for this title is available from
the British Library

All rights reserved. No part of this publication
may be reproduced, stored in a retrieval system,
or transmitted at any time or by any means
electronic, mechanical, photocopying, recording
or otherwise without the prior permission
of the copyright holder.

*The publisher works with the financial assistance of the
Arts Council of Wales*

Cover Photograph: 'The River Wye near Chepstow' by Barry Needle

Printed in Palatino by
WBC Book Manufacturers, Bridgend

Contents

I

- 9   Coda
- 10   Rain
- 11   East and West
- 12   South Wales
- 13   The First Severn Bridge
- 14   Mind Wandering in the Barbican
- 15   The Widower
- 16   She Wrote to Me

II

- 23   A Third Place
- 26   Global Warning
- 27   Environmentalists
- 28   Grains of Sand
- 29   Their Only Bliss
- 30   When We Were Young
- 31   Liber Mundi
- 32   Almost Touch It
- 33   Late Thoughts in March

III

- 41   Follow the Foliage
- 42   Student Prince
- 43   Near Rhossili
- 44   Gatwick: Planes Landing and Leaving
- 45   Harvest
- 46   Vocation
- 47   An Abortion
- 48   Independence

IV

53 Hallucination
54 The Second Son
55 For Their Own Good
56 April
57 Dunblane
58 A Later Poet (Maybe Tu Fu)
    Reads the Quiet One
59 Word Work
60 Nativity
61 Poem for Abertawe

72 *Acknowledgements*

I

Coda

Always, the leaf-driving
wind and lashing rain to rattle
doors and bring branches, twigs to drop
on roads to snap there and be raddled equally
and the silence of this house, my wrists'
movement audible as I write, and my
thoughts so too.

A sidelong moon has grey cloud flung
across it like lace curtain for a
watcher outside, a path's flat
slabs wet-shining to a cottage door, with
dark panes besides, as from the drawing of
a child, and the child inside, cold white
hands round a teacup, remembering, alone.

There were two sheepdogs as I walked
in the hail and under the lane's electric
light, but one is missing now, I call and
call but still he does not come, the
other's tousled wispy hair, slinks with
me as a car passes, with sugary
whiff of gasoline.

Back in the house, fists on chin and
thought, thought, thought. The moon
cracked autumn branches centuries ago;
it will again; the village's lights
flick on at tea-time one by one and falling
leaves handwrite across the grass;
we will not change, we will not change

Rain

Great walls of mist moved inland
From estuary to woods, cupfuls of water
Cataracted from the drain-pipe, spewed
On the lawn and the dog's
Wet coat gripping him, hung snarling
To him till he shivered and slunk off.
The turned earth seeped, the radio's
Classical music trilled alongside
The wind's storm. A man was alone,
Was ready to write and he wrote, lurching
On sound not footprints as one might through snow.

He sat at a table as on a moor,
His elbows two rocks. Thinking
Was thanking that amalgam of ruined wind, of
Winter leaves like paint-brushes or dead
Crows in trees; of flapped, flicked rain.
The black-and-white dog was now a dot.
To think had always been bedlam,
Images too fast for facts' contingencies,
Like tools oiled carefully in a shed, that he
Might use, or they use him; to feel
The last green year there, the branches
And cumulus of the sky, but that seasons
Too caused gale in their four orders.

East and West

The roused storm grabs the trees' long hair
Like a psychopath, going for Heathrow and London.

Vans and coaches crawled the other way.
They bashed and ripped along the motorway.

Hailstones pocked the platform at Swindon.
The HST barged its whale's snout on.

The wind swept up from St David's Head.
All saints and sinners cower in bed

Tonight, if they've got any sense.
The hurricane seethes up channel by France,

And it still has that black, single voice
I hear. No romantic now, but there's no choice.

At home it smashed the cross beam in the barn.
We repaired it with the oak it blew down.

South Wales

(for MC)

His eyes melted and rotated
All round my head but never at it.
Like a face seen through a squalled windscreen
Or like stopped wrist-watch faces.
One eyeball shot up into his head.
The other was a sort of marble.

We read out the great Milton stanzas
And he tilted his head
As though listening for a salt wind
Down channel, or a distant foghorn sound.
It was really so important to help.
The Cork ferry smoothed across the waters.

I must be blind, or something.
(At the back of the desk diary:
*Caring and concern. Work for
Partial Vision Unit. Get hospital Info.*)
An evening a week. Say Tuesdays.
Or deaf to incoming signals.

The First Severn Bridge

Up to its paying turnpike, towed
In cars like beetles veering the road,
Across the huge arc tensed and bowed,
We tourist drivers glanced up, awed.

Enormous bobbins taper down.
Cables bear their stanchions' strain.
Trusses grip their blocks' foundation.
Rockers stress all loads to one.

The flat crown is a liner's deck.
Thunk, and a vast container truck
Slots in behind the next car back.
Far out the holm sleeps in its rock.

Hell, bridge, does any one of us
Not feel non-being under us?
What sort of being hung like this?
Constructed to outstare our gaze.

Mind Wandering in the Barbican

A tall, acoustic aery space
With angled cliffs of concrete wall.
The instrumentalists air sounds,
The audience attends in rows.

But down in Wales a swaying tree
Flails, waves its arms, conducts the sea,
The cliff a staircase to the sands.
He had ten fingers but no hands

And shook them out as though to spin
The water off. The first violin
Punched up the air like a shark's fin,
The cellos leapt like dolphins in

A surf-board championship. At home
We played the tape. Splendidly
The same concerto came across
Just like a visitor had come.

The Widower

He tramped and climbed on colossal
Heights above Brecon not having seen
How blank they were or that his widower's
House so far below would look

So small. He walked them daily
Sixteen years, somehow sure
She'd died a mere month back and he
Should do some project for a while.

April one year he met up there
Another lady, trekking, middle-aged.
After a walk they planned tea-trysts.
And once she came, and then she didn't come.

Only then the sun ablazed.
Oranges, jets, double-decker buses,
Oriental girls, wine bars, violins,
On the black hill, as it is named.

She Wrote to Me

one

Thirteen Canada-geese flew over
But one seemed to split, which thus made
Fourteen. Every night my dream
Was of being pinned to a ledge,

Whether office-block or sheer cliff,
And the vertical height made my gut
Sag, and there was no centre of gravity
Left for me. On the new mobile phone

I tried to call up, them to pull me up
But the sound went down, pulling my
Eyeballs after it. Gorgeous red
Trees and fields lay calmly

Before us and then turned green.
Oh that the earth could again be green.
Nevermore. The flat spin of the stars
Returned and that was all my grace.

two

I bought a flat, near the cathedral walls
Whose moat was a kind of ring-road now
For all these days. There was no coal fire,
So we walked and walked, breathing

The pasture's air, the deep hang-glider
Wafting across like a moth to burnish his song.
Into the snow the handpicked tourists marched,
Playing their disks and paying their bills,

The President's term still not up. But
Across the sea, where the rugby games were played,
A huge bird, a colossal eagle soared,
And I named it "Cobalt Blue" for itself,

There being no pair, whereby it might seed
A further again. Maybe the furniture knew,
Or the tall radio towers that grew like trees,
Shedding their bulletins like autumn leaves.

three

After the night, when the new pen was delivered,
I made a box for paints, and kept the song
In a plastic wrapper, as the gardening manuals
Decreed. There was simply no time,

The years had sprinted away, round the last bend,
And the Jumbo's gold had climbed its stair
Up to that stratosphere where Plato worked,
Filling his diary, having his chocolate drink

At eleven. Into the Gothic church
The cavalry rode, their liveries green
As the new-tipped grasses built on Easter day.
A cabinet meeting broke up, order

Maintained as was its womanly wont,
For these are the days, when everything
Is decided once and for all, the electronic
Machine is might, and tells, and is invisible.

four

Delightfully the T-shirt and the jeans
Swing on the line and show their subtle arts
Caressing the flesh they espouse. Only a man
Going skywards in an elevator-express

Could doubt the instants of the coffee bean,
The unbought share, the caravan where
The great waves break and swim breathlessly
Ashore. A giraffe appeared at that

Point, slowly gyrating its huge
Opinions and then dodged gracefully away.
A serpent slid back down its tube, which
It fitted exactly. My domestic camera

Quietly advises me not to say a word,
In case some solicitor hears, and starts
To trapeze, as people will when happiness
Jumps unexpectedly, on the new-mown grass.

five

We need a word for *God* and there isn't one.
So maybe quiet is real, or the very sound
Of grass scraping on sand, billowing the air's
Pollution we've come to hold and not unmake.

Jesus the bit that died, his blood trickling
As from someone killed in a crash, the driver mad
With fast-lane speed, his sperm shot
From an overwrought mind where big cats hugged

In outer space, that outer, outer space,
Where science pours its neutralizing hopes,
Announcing in print the crazy possibilities
No one chose and no one else would have known,

The letters all sent in pillar-box red
To destinations we don't even know are there.
Others turned into mice, dogs into men,
The creation blazoned with bread, chance and dream.

six

The gold they valued, longer lasting than truth,
Unrusting like iron, unbending like lead,
Beautiful as urine or the spring primrose,
Where I carved a destroying meat and ate

My fill. Even the tortoise can't overturn
In its shell, and then go right side up
Like a kayak used in fitness sports.
The screens danced to the conductor,

The announcer rattled the evening facts
While with his hidden left hand
Reached to the side for the curdled drink
In which the mixing girl had put more gin

Than an unbuilt reservoir intended for the rain
We let slip to the seaside, year by year
Still cleaning our priceless teeth, those
Exquisite gems, through which to tell our hearts.

seven

She wrote to me, I knew that hand,
Spindly and sweet, like a child's favourite sky.
At the motorway halt we had soup, and kept
All the free coupons, my bank so grateful, while

Fourteen men, each the line of a sonnet, lit
Their taboo nicotine and started their trek
Up the cold glacial slopes. Their green
Coats mirrored the last constellations

The space-probe would ever reach. Crying
The women lay on the ground, a black
Baby was born and it shall never die. Frogs,
Jumping into the pond, were so persuasive

In how to swim for the best, not to mind
Their lot or imagine that becoming princes
Would pay off the mortgage or clean
The mess from the hills, for work and love.

eight

The vehicles drove to the nub, a centripetal
Starfish, cheering the heart. When they returned
It was dusk, and people toasted their scones
On specially-heated air. A schoolgirl ran

Across the park to her door at this time,
Chased of course, but no one else would
Have known her name's derivation, or that
It was etched on silver in her purse,

A grandma's gift. Blue the huge colour,
Snow the moment that stayed, and a wounded man,
Rebelling against the armaments a government
Sent, stared at the poppies that grew

On his legs and chest. Even the roundabout spun,
But the tune it played on that cranky old
Machine gave out more teams than a dictionary,
Hung on the garden tree for a thousand years.

II

A Third Place

Its crackling unsubtle hugeness under snow
And like for some panoramic camera that pink glow
Redeemed are for me the underpinning thought
And first colour. I've been years away now

From that packed, spaced-out and all-season ranch.
Indian, Saxon, Eskimo and French
Were its forced peoples, and the one thin red-hot
Railroad had pushed and carved as though for every inch

Of track by dynamite-blasting excavation.
That route bought its figure-of-eight elevation
From the mountain ranges with such locomotive sweat
Of gross energy as to attempt a single nation

Thought geographically impossible. To me
It has all deepened and unified merely
To the irreducibly perceived; what cannot
Now be other than past, unshiftable reality.

A lifetime back I did live there. I see towns of maples
Lilting in tuneful avenues, and clap-board steeples
On pioneer churches and transcontinental freight
Shunting through the snow on greens, purples

And whites of mountain-sides. Naturally it seemed
An incomplete culture then, that what many deemed
Generations earlier an uncertain thing,
Must still stay out there beyond reach in such untamed

Lake-pocked forest and silent low-slung prairie,
Plain and distance. And the sky, past wiry
Telegraph-cables over littered ghost-town streets,
Simply underlined my own incomplete mind and pure
                                                memory.

In one summer for instance we built a cabin by
Our cottage, in the spruce trees and firs as high
As Canada-geese, us smacking nails down
Knotted timber that smelt of soap and felt as dry

As snuff. The sun on us swung brilliantly between
Clefts of sticky and spiky black branches seen,
As if magnified, through a lens to ignite pulp but
To warm chipmunk and squirrel as well, balm the
                                        evergreen.

In one fall we drove for days among yellow leaves
And blood-red ones, and had near shaves
Just missing trucks at *No U-Turn* signs. Girls perched
On our knees, we swam in their one-season loves.

In one winter I bought a hockey-stick
And on collapsing ankles had thrills sending the puck
Frictionless down plains and terrains of ice
Like travelling, scored some goals (by luck)

Then licked all my bleeding knuckles. I took
A college course and in vacations work
In a spatter of jobs, department store
Assistant, lifeguard, railway-diner cook

And then reception-clerk at the lush Lake Louise
Hotel where to a dark lawn lay that turquoise
Stretch of sheer water under a sky all ink-bottle blue.
Such memories. Such splinters of broken-glass memories

From a baggy, shapeless land, that strip
Of rock then snow then town then pine then trap,
Set by trappers in the bush for moose, fox and deer.
That jagged territory pegged out like a map

Seems now mere selectivity and randomness.
And there is, too, the present need to reduce
All I wondered and felt, all my ideology
To the rawest of mineral, wood, and furs,

Which the indigenous were making then in the new way.
Rising conceptions, techniques and arts to array
And renew their essence as they now proliferate
Just on three thousand miles and currents away.

For I'll never live there again now. They're gone times.
But to recall, by night or day, such stirring names —
"Great Bear Lake, Yellowknife, Fort Resolution" —
It races the pulse, brings back a couple of dreams.

Global Warning

(announcement of 2,000 scientists, 16 October 1995)

Nothing left to revere then,
No nature beyond our meddlings,
Night the preferred medium, as though
Noon's sun gave merely a mode

For electricity to make seem
Folly in transit. Now looking at those
Forests and veldts we shall never
Feel again, we are finally

Here, us to ourselves at last.
Hopefully the remainders will be docile.
Hooray (amplified) some shout, emitting
Halitosis; well done, humans.

Well done humans. Language
Wakes up with a start. Galaxies start
Whirling backwards yet seem not
Wrong. Babies are insanely beautiful.

Environmentalists

Pollution is our religion.
People not. Watch it though for
Perhaps it is risky to deflect

Love. Which would be best
Let's ask, a world crammed by
Lusts our loves become, or one

Emptied, a coke-clinker spinning?
Either is void but these two
Evils could have different outsets.

I say only that love's total
Is no number. A dozen humans
In love are still love infinite.

Where, third planet, are you
Wandering, how may we travel to
Win you, when shall we arrive?

Grains of Sand

Grains of sand, owl eggs, long rye
Grasses not yet scythed, even blue
Germs or cells humans came from and so
Go back to instead of what only
Guarantees the useful: what can be

Done. Now it seems I must
Drive as fast as cheetahs
Dash at night, to be clean must
Drain rivers, I must glut all
Desire. Such life modulates each

Substance known for its action now
Seen as consumed, not met
So as to know it. If these cars
Signal some deeper pattern or end they
Surge up from , we must soon

Feel such from their slipstream or
Foot to the floor happily, or
From the poor ladybirds they copy.
Further planning is useless: go
Farm: count chickens: hairs numbered.

Their Only Bliss

The tanker crashes on the rock.
Titanic oozes leave the hull
That slowly crumbles in its shock.
The strait was soon a lake of oil.

Society cracks open too,
Seeping its billion children out.
Soon the race must overflow,
Saturate the only planet.

And all the wars (like Bosnia)
Are less than zero next to this.
Alphabets of skins and hair
Arranged in death, their only bliss.

When We Were Young

When we were young we
Were part of this same
World as turns now.
Where did it go?

Suddenly it's not just
Small but curiously
Sensitized. We can
Sound off unknown places.

Africa's a dark poster.
Asia teems with dots.
Antarctica's a negative.
Australia skis on sand

In technicolour.
Is this some new store of
Information or do
I just know myself?

Maybe next we'll
Motivate *Who is*
My neighbour in
More subtle definition.

Liber Mundi

We last persons are letters of
Words we cannot read and science
Will not mistake. The book of this
World turns its sunlit pages,

Night on night, twenty-four hours each
New dawning. They are filling up.
Now there is such knowledge that
Nations melt like snow, text reappears.

It Is Written, it said. What is?
I am Alpha and Omega meant just so:
In The Beginning will be concluded.
Ink is irrigation's foaming dark:

Our light both truth and sun,
Only the laboratory's white coat
Or hygienic dancing enamel
Occasions the global charm

That might go two ways, one or
The other. Will the great opus be
Tragedy again, or are some genres
Taught to effect on the radio waves?

Almost Touch It

Given that such exists clearly
Goodness placed us here not somewhere else.
Goodness not space is the medium
Granted for beings to breathe of, while to
Go mad in a void is not intelligent.

Maybe the emptiness (distance
Millions of clones of earth could never
Make up) is what it says. Not
"Miles and miles and miles" etc but
Mere nothing; not; just not; strange

Relation between spots that hang heavy.
Radiation must find trajectory and then
Reach splashdown through blue drops of air.
Rich pasture mellows below. Friends
Resolve to help, it's how they are and

The ether occupies the only
Territory to outweigh matter on its own
Terms. Some days you can almost
Touch it, as sweet as grass and as
Tender as the skin of whoever you love.

Late Thoughts in March

It is Good Friday. Good.
Liturgy at seven in the hasped church,
Vigil till midnight. The village incensed.
A pagan cross. A Celtic stone.

How lovely are the motorways,
They bring us the gospel of peace.
Chickweed and plantain swept tidily back
To the soft verge like a hairdo
Servicing the creche's green needs.
Our cars the cursor's arrows.
The motorway enables,
The motorway knows.

On the pre-birth shore,
The salt unfilmed, the wave ski-ing in,
Its crash a greatcoat wrapped round me.
We shouldn't have left;
The sea air and chlorine gorse
Submerging the mind,
Below the water-line it sinks
Out of the range of cameras.
On this coast the white stones
Like ostrich eggs turned by the sea
For millennia — a model
That any laser-beam cutter
Now does far better,
With enough subtle variation
To emulate nature's quiddity
By whatever design-technology
Sent Nature to such force-lines
That little remains to do
Bar monitor the emotions
Of the six billion psyches;
Breathe, manifest, consume.

*

Now it is midnight. Shoals of rain.
The sea wind snaps the lavender stalks,
It levels the grass to the path's concrete.
No snow-hatted mountain ranges,
No ocean-plates in turmoil,
No disturbance of radiation,
No stellar collapse or galactic pulses,
No flood of sperm to the ova
Can now stay unknown, in binary not renderable,
For every newborn infant
Squelching from between the legs
At eleven thousand a minute
Is one more inch of distance from those things.

Brine more oil than plankton,
Mussels and whelks rotted,
The village's lawns plastic,
The greenhouse door inflatable,
No land stays not finger-marked
By "developmental increments",
From "Nature" such mean, Nature itself that mean,
Chemico-reduced, extracted,
Sponsored, covenanted, designed,
Jets stinging like summer flies,
Squads of tourists in the welkin.

The globe not infinity but a compound,
The saturation of the terrains,
The sudden eruption of the populations,
The buzzing like locusts through the airspace,
The bucketings of the drainings of the water,
The roads that connect roads that connect roads,
And all to become a film of itself,
The audience the cast and the directors.
Where is our thanks to the heathen?

Who had no fridges, no switches, no tapwater,
Who clenched their fists on their brainwork
At day and night or on the killingfield,
Ensuring, merely, that we got here
Where now we are, locked, fenced in and timeless.

What if Earth lives
As Gaia thinks? Then it needs
Attention like all living things.
Undesired by its lilywhite moon,
Spinning distractedly some distance
From any conceivable companion,
Head sadly in its hands,
We are its jagged nerves,
Its catachresis, its identity problem,
We are its skin disease,
Poisoning its foods, trimming its lovely woods,
Injecting its drugs, inducing our own fissions,
Contaminating its air and its foodstuffs,
And multiplying ourselves in that disarrangement.

*

And this our exact and most rightful end,
The *telos* where the primeval sludge
Was always pointed and aimed.
The quick gap of the "Nature" thing,
The cow's eyes shining in the buttercups,
The trout stream asleep in the meadow,
The "tang of sea salt"
The "peat floor of the forest"
The raindrop's path down the window-pane,
Each a twitch on the planet's football-mango,
As we enter "phase total enervation"
And probable concomitant,
Centripetal implosion, paradoxical knot,
Inward tangles of interravelled expansion.

*

*

*

Hold your panic, friend. Calm it.

*

Calm it.

*

There's nothing whatever to fear.
On this soft coast at least, tonight,
The tanks and lambs are silent,
The smashed bodies elsewhere.
The bottles nestle in the rock-pools,
The gentle folk walk along the sand dunes,
Seaweed still tangs on the stretched sand.
Mental disorder eases itself,
The pewtered sea-ripples levelled
Like gold wheat when the breeze lifts,
Gorse a candle
For dumped cars uncrashed,
Our existences scanned for.
"Whither is it gone?"
Beats us with its equation
As this woman busies in the garden
And rain trickles down her collar.
She shifts a snail along the brickwork
While a steel-eyed thrush, mindless
Of these theories, seeks its pang
Of hunger, like storm-clouds in Bosnia.
A stunted Bonsai tree (anagram)
Is her next-door neighbour,
Not well in himself the grocer's wife
Told us; knee-caps twisted inward,
Rickets, poorly invested, unprofitable.
Sex rolls its lustre
And the petrified TV screen blinks.

*

When the old write they write desperately,
Knowing experience bitter,
Advice useless if not tentative.
A huge tyre spins off its axle
Bombing the shale embankment,
Exciting magpies, crushing voles,
The trigger for civil war.
The knockout peels off her school uniform
And on page three becomes a tulip.
He shifts a slab in the garden.
Woodlice unwrap their neat parcels
And move off with dispatch.

*

Cooking fish he slashed his hand
On tinfoil: deep cut to the bone,
Blood-drops like the sea-anemone.
In Minor Casualty
The Pakistani nurse, with a doctorate,
Inserts exquisite embroideries.
He feels her tapping finger-ends.
Blackbirds' wings
Flap the pronged TV aerial
In the Atlantic mind rushing through me,
Up channel from the sea's
Chocolate waves, their boiling thrash
As cold as Greenland ice. A tuft
Is a green hedgehog and as wondrous.
When all these calamities
Cease and we lie down at length
In the cold earth's body-bags,
"Whither Is It Gone?"
Will be outstanding, you can just hear
The long sound of the planets
Continue their outward parabolas,
Always the measure of love.

III

Follow the Foliage

(for Morris and Sue Schopf)

An American philosopher
Wrote under trees, so it is said
In this encyclopedia.
Mauve, yellow, burnt sienna, red,
The autumn leaves fell round his head
Like fancies chasing round his head.
It was Thoreau. One day this man

Read how the Buddha picked some leaves,
And showed his followers and said
"The forest's foliage, next to these,
Is all the thoughts I could have said.
These were just some." Last year in Maine
All my New England colleagues said
Follow the foliage. So we did.

Next year we followed it again.
Hourly reports on radio
Broadcast the turning leaves. A day
Can set the maple trees on fire
In orange tongues, and from your car
You kind of see the waves recede
Like daylight full of clouds at speed

In wave on wave, a week or more
Chasing them up to Canada.
The birch leaf goes a rustier red.
The tulip leaf is like a spade.
I guess I'm no philosopher.
We saw a million leaves last fall
And no thought bothered us at all.

Student Prince

(for T and E)

We needed an older Claudius.
He was thirty-two.

Not ready for this,
From a "disease contracted
Vacationing" — and who could have known
That the A40 would be clogged,
Getting to the church on time
Choked at the sad end also,
The aisles empty when we reached them?

By the grave a young man
Was just finishing. Just patting down
Earth with trowel and hands
As we stood round too late
For service. He smiled brightly.
"Sinks in gradually" he said.
"When the rain stays off."

Now pile your dust upon the quick and dead.
Readiness all, however unexpected.

Near Rhossili

Inland gulls
    In a field's freshwater flood,
Cows too, fewer and far far heavier,
    Mingled on dripping grass and mud.
The mind eased and something lifted
    At this, as though a gentle draining
Where had been dammed
    Obstruction. Or perhaps the raining
That was grey and had just burdened me
    Was already gone with you, and I
Am alone too much out here and more
    Than is good for anyone, I don't know.
Away the gulls blow
    Like leaves, but they are so
White the experts think of snow.
    The search for carrion hurries on
Elsewhere out there, a city seen from the sky
    Must look like gulls, or swift
Planes on a landing strip
    Up the M4 from here, Heathrow
Or somewhere, I don't know.
    But I watch all this from a car
Then stop and slam the door, the gulls
    Look unabashed, the planet full,
The field's grass soon to be cemented
    Here or elsewhere for a site
For the handicapped or otherwise demented,
    Or office-block in a field, where gulls alight.
Once I saw them here in flocks
    Trailing a tractor's wake
In a ploughed field in full sail
    Picking at goodies in the earth's cake,
Not flung by any forecast gale,
    Eating for mere survival's sake.

Gatwick. Planes Landing and Leaving

Dots shine, they twinkle in the sun.
Then swell, descending from the clouds
A queue of dots, then land their shrouds
As though to skate the world is fun.
They come and come, out of the sun.

They track and taxi into place
Then charge, a sudden lurch of speed
Before their lift-offs into space.
Each a huge double-decker bus.
At every window-slot, a face.

Harvest

Oil-seed rape, wheat, barley, hay.
The wheat sunbathing like a door
Or swimmers laughing to the sea.

Poppies bespatter one whole field
As though a million English died.
A labrador bounds through the wheat

Like a Loch Ness monster, happily.
Pure butter clogs the motorway.
Corn ripples through the farm-girl's hair,

A block of flats rears in the corn.
The combine tows its factory on,
A yellowed buggy on the moon

Where silence is. The skylark's song
Rings like a telephone had rung
For hours with no one answering.

Vocation

A paper landed at their shoes.
It fluttered from the trees
And said to aid a falling world
Of affluence and ease
There are no unreplenished arts
That were not once applied
In eras of prehistory
When every loser died.

There was no panacea to give
Of skills the lonely man
Secreted in his words to drill
From his creative brain.
More than a generation back
They took the best-known route
Along the new-laid motorways
The maps now show complete.

All across the grass we sowed
Unwritten fragments lie,
Flakes of barum on the sills,
Grey snow in the sky.
All the ancient poems hang
Like game beneath the stairs
And every woman swings in fear
For every child she bears.

An Abortion

And he went to the inn, and out to
the building at the back, the decrepit stable,
and he had to know, if they were there, in the
quiet lofts, the cattle stalls, whether it
was true, and precisely what was true, and he
entered, to the glimmer of light, and the
noise of the inn, was nearby, yet he excluded it
completely, shut it out, and saw a small
shawled woman, and a thin man, an indecisive
one, and others with them, sheep tenders,
bearded, who were uncertain, unsettled and
afraid, he thought, and it was dark though,
cobwebby, despite the oxen's oaty breath, a
moth-eaten donkey, a camel, and a candle, and
a wooden trough, with straw in it, and they
all near it, and he, standing in dung, edging
forward, searching for it, saw it; a minute
foetus, a tiny white thing, not five inches
long, it had been untimely born, and he stared
and stared, and suddenly saw; it was alive, it
was not dead at all, it was its exquisite,
unimaginable and incredible self; and he,
quickened and amazed, ran out to the club, the
pub and the farmer's house, telling everyone there.

Independence

one

Where are you, England?
Where have you gone?
I miss you so.
I must ask my son,

He'll know. He rides
Hurriedly each day
Commuting the trains,
Crammed in the corridor

To Victoria and on,
Tired by his trek.
New grass in Hyde Park.
None on Scafell Pike.

two

Where are you England?
Where were you hiding?
Everyone so worried
Evening after evening.

You loved your motorbike.
Yes oh how we know.
Foot down knee up
Flashing the mainbeam there.

But a great danger
Burnt in our ears.
We were too many.
We miss those quiet hours.

three

England is merry.
Ecstasy time.
Wet at the quarry
Wind-surfers foam.

Inland they cream
In this gravel crater
Sure England's island
Surrogates this water.

Muscular butterflies,
Magnificent in sun.
O England so proud
Of your supermen.

four

The Wye turns its golden
Tresses along the soil.
Fertile waits its valley
For the cruising male.

It is green and half lost
In the casual haze.
Another country
Awaits these old borders.

Hills, curve and raise and
Heed us where we live.
Negotiating summer.
New moments to crave.

IV

Hallucination

Two boys playing on the lawn.
A modest lake left by the rain
Adorns the path beside the lane.
Upside-down the tree-trunks sink
Reflections for a staring man
To see himself in, flooded. Then,
Out from this deep hallucination,
Silent on the cottage lawn
In front of where we used to live
I see a tiny girl in pink.

Who is she? I know who she is.
The daughter that I never had.
I had two brothers and their dad
Was just an only, like his wife.
A kind of thin, one-gendered life.
My own wife's only sister died.
Two brothers ever at my side,
No girl. Ah, how I wondered who
She was or any like her was.
I stare down at the looking-glass.

The Second Son

Sons kill their fathers in their sleep.
Sleep with their mothers, it is said.
Sophocles wrote so. Freud the complexity.

But if the elder has murdered soon, shed
Blood already, what follows on?
By now the poor old git is slain.

Or wandering around with watery eyes
On Saturdays, watching the rugby perhaps.
On Sunday waits for opening hours.

Maybe a daughter should have been.
Mother and daughter not father and son.
Mad times at night reach for the stars.

Your question (am I my brother's keeper?)
Yearns and yearns for its hard answer.
Yes you are splashes across the water.

For Their Own Good

Dad, do I have to go away?
You'll feel OK in the morning I lied,

Drying his eyes with a baby boy's
Yukkie flannel. So long ago and

Distantly I see those cottage beds
Years back and how each night each

Day piled up to the time being
Young would fade. This final week,

Drunk with prizes, Old Boys and cricket,
Yesterday half-flickers back like some

Damp poster stuck to a wall,
Yellowing the paper. *Parties and*

Decisions and stuff Dad... work and New
York... don't fret... back in October...

Do you have to go away? All I can say.
Yawns of discernment. Optional now.

April

("COLIN MICHAEL PAICE
born 13th February 1957
Fell asleep on the SCAFELL PIKE
10th January 1976.
He Lived & Died Happily
On His Beloved Mountains."
St. Olaf's Church, Wasdale,
Smallest church in England.
Oak beams we could reach.
Bible open for a reading.)

We drove to Wasdale. Dreadful screes
Shot straight into the dirty lake
Like sunbeams, blacker slopes rose up
To Scafell Pike, a rage of snow
Blown over layers of frozen snow.

The mountain's face sheer like a board
Or hoarding, but he never wanted
My advice, just said "I'm going"
And humped his rucksack (birthday present)
And cake which did him for the present.

A group of climbers later spoke
To us, "We lost him". We trudged up
To Sty Head past the only church,
The crags confused the sky with vaults.
Great Gable smashed the range with vaults.

Ravines beside colossal cliffs
Were making emptiness of air
Beside them look an upright thing
Slung on vast hinges, beautiful
Like anything not beautiful,

Abrasive gullies, sudden ice
That stimulates the flesh itself.
We thought high up a boulder moved.
Seems he had peaked, then ambled down.
We got to him, glad he was down.

Dunblane

We need our children to remain children.
These few will do that for us.

When we die they will still live.
The small bright faces on the sideboard.

Why is our earth out of joint?
There is an answer but not here.

Weeping just audible, near silent.
Threat, torment, fear have the tongue.

Women bear, and then they bear.
To die at four being not thinkable.

Waifs, petals, feathers.
Tiny things, intercede for us.

A Later Poet (Maybe Tu Fu) Reads the Quiet One

The words of Wang Wei:
From his example I
 Endeavour order

First I place my lady
Then her children surely
 As they teach

Procrastination rife
Essential to the cultured life
 I learn such

Smiling, curious
Then look to my house
 Its clapperboards

Flawless in motive
Flush in work and love
 Obdurate

My folk will I bury
Gifted and decently
 At the time

Against ill-luck to come
With order their own
 And their own music

Word Work

Badly I need you, you, and that
Body you gave me when I gave myself.

Windows are where you always stand,
Wondering if even summer rain is heaven.

Live as us both, whenever die,
Love still recedes and won't be named.

Sing like you did, but just for me,
Songs we recall, but not the day.

Are we? Is? The question and alone
Air undressing all you have become.

Nativity

Would you like my breast, she said.
No more than the rest, he said.

Will there be no speech, she said.
Once into the breach, he said.

Shall we have a babe, she said.
Tested in the tube, he said.

Will the sun explode, she said.
If we overload, he said.

I'm your equal now, she said.
Here's the sequel now, he said.

Watering the plants, she said,
Future at a glance, he said.

She: I am essential earth.
He: I follow in your path.

Poem for Abertawe

Mud, Humber and gull.
Serene discourses
On poetry's jail,
The middle-classes.
Academe still
Emends its bending phrases.

Collegiate hall,
Tall red-brick tower.
"Adequate" hotel.
Bathroom and shower.
A pinging bell,
Peanuts on the bar,

Big names at the party.
One rowdy lot
Arty and farty.
Some I thought
Were literati.
They were not.

(I, I, says the poem,
I this, I that.
Aye-aye goes the train,
Rat-a-tat, rat-a-tat.
Our individualism
Ended like that?)

In lecture-rooms
With rising tiers
(No pun), new names,
And sensate peers
Punching out themes
With fists and airs;

Crude, hardly real,
Such conference.
So inimical,
So intense.
Politics is all
Each speaker rants —

Or felt as much.
Untrue, unjust.
Most sought to reach
A halfway trust
Where human speech
Survived the dust —

And this godawful train.
In floods, borne west
A flat grey fen
Of windmill waste
To Gilberdyke, down
And rolling fast

Inland to Goole
And Doncaster.
No way to tell
How being there
Occurred at all
Or where we were.

*

Larkin had Dockery.
Some have sons.
Should we have quit,
Become proletarians?
They wouldn't have had me,
With such opinions.

A coffee soaks
The formica by
The train's jerks.
The steward's fly
Undone, the jokes
(He can't see why)

As the train jogs.
A shame to write
Of fens, bogs
And approaching night
In wandering mazes,
Milton's lost sight

In the corridor.
A mum yells loud
Because I effing tell yer!
Semiotic code
On the linguists' view.
Just like they said.

And like that thing
Of Heidegger's.
We speak no tongue,
The tongue speaks us.
When we were young
No one said this

In Yorkshire vowels
Dispensing soup
Or paper towels
Or BR soap.
Half-heard denials
That time is up.

*

A train oncoming.
Its orange lights
And quick passing
Like sudden insights,
Headlines seething
For ephemeral rights —

Flat country.
A temporary reprieve.
In a dark sky
Live and let live
As though the free
Opposed the Slav,

And thinking that way
We aren't so much,
It had to be
The middle-class such
As my lot knew
Was a social hotch-potch,

Each a new freak,
By which I mean
I'd sooner look
At some bird on the train
Of consumerist stock
And media-addled brain,

The old problem there
He'd always had
Of the verbal layer
To a clergyman Dad
And a neurotic Ma
Who did nothing bad.

(Oh my father
Where are you?
Oh my very dear mother,
Who told you
That we knew better,
That we knew, that we knew?)

       *

The train's noises
Amble and purr
Through the deep Midlands,
Its thin car
And neon-strips
Our habitat now,

Its iron rattling
Under a bridge
Entering a cutting.
Frictional nudge
Of points setting
Beneath the carriage.

We stopped at Sheffield.
We changed there.
Next stop Chesterfield
In Derbyshire.
Soon Lichfield.
Three spires where

Johnson aspired.
Peaks to the sky
And a reservoir's head.
The potteries' industry
Here was once chimneyed.
Black Country,

Though now at last
Black doesn't mean
Something not racist
But something not green,
Our exploited places,
Our unkempt scene,

Each town another.
All black all night.
We trundle over
The unspeakable sight
Of a canal's saliva.
Its spit, its shit.

*

Larkin, poet.
Some said the best.
One poem he wrote
By train, possessed.
Now in the night
Of time at least.

Douglas Dunn, poet.
His need to give
Magnificent heart
Because of love.
Grief's light
Placed on her grave.

Andrew Marvell, poet.
MP for Hull.
Their peer laureate.
Well Andrew Marvell,
Was it on, being poet
And MP as well?

We hit the blaze
Of a basement station.
This is New Street.
Platform, lights, din
Of doors and feet.
Supporters climb on.

Wave their scoreline,
Sit where I sit,
Books and alone.
There you have it.
Villa two Spurs one
Crap poetry nought.

Through a tunnel's tubes
We glide away
Sloughing off suburbs
Behind and sway
Through the wood's ribs
In Worcestershire country,

Genteel and true,
Malvern and on,
With Edward Elgar
English of tune
And Cheltenham Spa.
The old refrain.

*

Poetry refrains
From ideologies.
Poetry constrains,
Says what it says.
In power-drunk zones
It rots and frays.

And if population
Don't read the stuff?
Human condition.
They've had enough
Of education.
The rough dole's rough.

More true: we are dupes.
We are food and fear.
We are millennium babes.
Fast food, canned beer.
Bytes, logo-probes
Of the one idea.

We are globally warm.
We are two-pronged forks.
We are the bloom
On unrooted stalks.
We are Clinton's dream.
We are television talks.

We are Darwin's tribe
Seeded far away.
We are worldwide web,
We are superhighway.
We are tissue-blob.
We are DNA.

Parkway. Change
For an HST
Where Brunel's flange
Ran by the sea,
His steamboats plunged
Past Wales to America,

Bypassing the Cymry.
New business here,
New industry,
New art, new culture,
Brand new economy
In a Wales gone new.

Offa's neo-ciphers,
Japanese on lease,
Pot-holers, ex-wifers,
Weekenders named Rees,
Alternative-lifers
Dreaming of peace

As our train skirts lights
In necklace lines
Through terraced streets
In towns where tons
Of the black stuff sits
Unshifted, mines

Tamped down for ever. Shimmer
Of masts upside-down
In a greying river,
The structured town
Of Gwent's murmur
As night comes on.

*

Poems too have weaned
Themselves from myth.
Celtic and Saxon,
Both are both,
Sweet birds of Rhiannon
Left from our youth

When bird and angel
Flew from the dark.
Now the three birds' triangle
Brushing the ark
Of her face's oval
Never looks back

To this drizzling land,
Tract where I work,
Can't understand
These works you speak — ?
Yet have you for friend,
Stuck on the rock

Febrile, fertile,
Mud shore around
The sea's long wall
And waves that bind
It all, us all,
A deep tide turned

Where each self feels
Its best illusion.
All on the rail's
Departure and return
Of nature's force
I am one. We are one.

The tang of sea
And some pollution
Where to half be.
Ugly, lovely town.
Terminate here.
Write it all down.

Acknowledgements

Some of these poems have appeared in the following:

Anglo-Welsh Review, Brangle, English, The Interpreter's House, Magma, New Welsh Review, Poetry Nottingham, Poetry Review, Poetry Wales, The Rialto, Social Work Today, Swansea Review, Thumbscrew and the anthology *Picture: Welsh Poets.*